I wanna tell you
my story

I wanna tell you my story

DENISE BOWLES: DENBO

Story Terrace

Text Emily Richards, on behalf of StoryTerrace

Design StoryTerrace

Copyright © Denise Bowles and StoryTerrace

First print January 2022

StoryTerrace

www.StoryTerrace.com

For Mum.

I hope I've made you proud

CONTENTS

PROLOGUE

Why Am I Telling This Story?

So. You've picked up this book, you've seen my name is 'Denbo' and you know that I want to share my story with you. But *why* do I want to tell you this story, and why have I decided to tell it now?

Well, my life has been far from easy. I was diagnosed with a learning disability in my twenties - a label which has helped me to make sense of a childhood which was rife with academic struggles, relentless bullying, and frequent social isolation. I am also a survivor of childhood abuse, having spent five years of my teens living with a stepfather from hell. Not only this, but my twenties brought their share of challenges too: I faced deep struggles with my mental health, finding myself out of work and almost homeless. Finally, I am a lesbian. This last fact is, in fact, a source of great pride in my life today, and it gives me a great sense of fulfillment and belonging to be a member of the LGBT+ community. However, as a young person, coming to terms with my sexuality felt like yet another challenge for me to face. I had struggled so much to be accepted, and this felt like yet another struggle.

All of this being said, my life today is far from tragic. In fact, I'm the happiest I've ever been. I have meaningful work, where I draw upon my lived experience in order to make a difference to the lives of vulnerable people in my community. I have a great circle of friends and family, and a busy social life. I've even developed a following as a music artist, and have regular opportunities to perform on stage. I'm also a proud member of the LGBT+ community, and regularly attend pride marches across the UK and beyond.

So why do I want to tell you my story? Because I believe that it's a story of hope. Sometimes, when I look back at how far I've come over the years, and how much better things have gotten for me, I can hardly believe it. If only I had known back then how much better things would get, I might have found it a little easier to bear. So I'm telling my story in the hope that it might help somebody. Perhaps somebody, reading this, has been a victim of bullying or abuse themselves. Perhaps one of you is struggling with your sexuality, or with a learning disability diagnosis which seems like a life sentence. If that person is you, I say: don't lose hope. The world can be a cruel place but there are good people and good opportunities out there, waiting for you to find them. If, while reading this story, even one person is inspired to feel more hopeful about themselves or their life, I'll know that mine was a story worth telling.

1
EARLY CHILDHOOD

I was 2 years old, here, with blonde hair

My very first memory is from when I was four years old, attending Charlotte Street Nursery in Ilkeston. I recall that myself and the other children were sitting in a circle and our teacher, Mrs Jackson, had asked each and every one of us to tell her what we wanted to do that day.

I remember standing up, looking at the expectant little faces of my classmates and being totally stumped.

"Oh, I don't know." I said.

"Alright, never mind." Mrs Jackson replied, kindly. "I'll come back to you in a little while."

I sat back down and Mrs Jackson turned her attention to a little girl called Amanda. To this day, the image of Amanda standing up to answer the teacher's question remains vivid in my mind. Amanda was wearing a dress and had her hands plunged deep into its pockets, and she was absent mindedly swinging from side to side.

"I'm going in the doll's house, I am!" She declared, confident as can be.

"Ah," replied Mrs Jackson, in her warmly maternal voice, "and who would you like to take with you to play in the doll's house?"

Amanda turned to look at me with wide eyes. "Denise!" She announced.

Well, I thought to myself, *I suppose I'm playing in the doll's house!*

The rest, as they say, is history: Amanda and I remain good friends to this day.

***

Although I spent the first few years of my life in Beeston, the first home that I remember living in was No. 29 Peveril Drive in Ilkeston. I lived there with just my mum - Catherine - and my dad - Michael - until my younger brother - Martin - came along, five years later. I remember bragging to Amanda when Martin was born.

"I've got a baby brother!" I announced, proudly.

"Yeah," replied Amanda, thoroughly unimpressed, "well I've already got one!"

Even to this day, I can remember every detail of that house: the garden which led into the living room; the L shaped layout; the spiral staircase. Most of all, I remember my bedroom. It was only a little box room, but it was my private sanctuary and I adored it: the walls featured strips of bright pink paint at the top and the bottom, my bed was adorned with a My Little Pony duvet and the walls were lined with my collection of Troll Dolls and Care Bears. Describing all of this, I sound like a bit of a 'girly girl', but to this day I have never played with a Barbie doll!

There was in fact a fifth member of our household: a black labrador called Lady. Lady came into our lives in a slightly unusual way. At the time, Dad was working at a place called Manor Industrial Estate, and they had a guard dog: Lady. The Industrial Estate was eventually shut down and, when it was, nobody knew what to do with Lady. Being a guard dog,

Lady wasn't exactly the friendliest of dogs. Except, that is, with my mum. Mum would drop by every lunchtime to give my dad his sandwiches, and Lady would always greet her like an old friend. So, when Lady's tenure as a guard dog came to an end, she moved in with us to enjoy a leisurely retirement.

It would be remiss of me, when talking about my family, not to mention my grandparents. After all, they were a huge part of my life growing up, and I wouldn't be where I am today without them.

On my dad's side, there was Nana Mary and Grandad Don. When I was a teenager, I found out that Grandad Don was actually my dad's stepdad, and I met my biological grandfather, Grandad Bowles. Even still, Grandad Don remained a Grandad in my eyes. I'd see him and Nana Mary every other Saturday, when we'd drive over to their house in Carlton - which also seemed to be filled with various cousins - for a cup of tea and a chat.

Nana Mary and Grandad Don, on my dad's side

On my mum's side, there was Granny Rose and Grandad Micky. Of all of them, I was closest to Granny Rose. It has been over a decade since she left this earth, but I still miss my phone calls with her. I miss her getting the prayers out on the bed at night, and how she would grab me and press the prayers against my head. I miss going to the Saturday market with her and Grandad Micky: we would go there every fortnight and I'd always be treated to an ice cream in the summer months. Afterwards, we'd always get our tea from the fish and chip shop: Jacko's Chippy. To this day, it's still run by the same guy, Dennis. We'd get the works: fish, chips, mushy peas, curry sauce, bread, butter and a can of pop. You name it, we had it. In the winter months, we'd have Irish stew. Grandad would always be put in charge of the spuds, and he'd always overestimate how many he needed.

Granny and Grandad Rose and Mickey, on my mum's side

"Rosie," I can remember him saying, as if it were yesterday. "Have we got enough spuds here?"

"Jesus, Micky." My Granny would reply. "You've got enough to feed the whole street there!"

More often than not, that's exactly what we'd end up doing. Grandad would be on the phone, calling round the family, telling them to come over for their dinner: "we've got plenty of spuds to get through!"

It wasn't just Granddad Micky who had food mishaps, though. I came home one day to see Granny Rose halfway through making a trifle. As soon as I entered the door, as she always did, Granny peppered me with questions.

"How are you doing Denise? How was your day? What've you been up to?"

All the while, she was pouring glug after glug of sherry into her trifle: it was enough to tranquilise a horse, let alone a small Catholic lady! Granny Rose gave me the blame for that one - probably because Granddad Micky wasn't around to take the rap!

All jokes aside, I owe a huge deal to my grandparents. I lived with them on and off for twenty-three years and it's no exaggeration to say that - without the love and support that they showed me - I don't think I'd be around today to tell my story.

Photoshop with My Granny Rose

***

After a few years, my parents decided that they wanted an end house instead of a terrace, so we moved out of 29 Peveril Drive to No. 65 on the same road. This house had a much bigger kitchen, and, since I'd been lumped with the box room in our previous house, I got to have a much bigger bedroom this time round. I don't have many memories from our time at this house, except for the fact that I used to have a mischievous habit of writing and drawing pictures on the walls. Needless to say, I got in plenty of trouble for tarnishing the spotless magnolia paint with my artistic creations!

After finishing at Charlotte Street Nursery, I moved on to Granby Junior School, a little way further up the hill, and I settled in well there. My early years had their ups and downs, like anybody's. For the most part though, I had a happy childhood: I loved my family, I enjoyed school and I had good friends. That was all set to change though, when we moved to a new town and my happy little life was changed for good.

It was October of 1992, the autumn leaves just starting to redden and fall from the trees, when we moved to Eastwood. I was ten years old and Martin was only four. The reason for our moving was that Mum and Dad had split up, and Mum had met somebody else. It was a relationship that would last for five and a half years - including two years of marriage - and, frankly, it was a living hell for Martin and me. I felt

as though my whole world had turned upside down: I'd
lost my lovely home, my comfortable home town, my local
friends and my dad. I felt as though I didn't know who I was
anymore. The worst part of it all was that I had to change
schools, and that was where the bullying began.

I was in Year 6 when I began at Lyncroft Primary School.
It was a difficult age to start at a new school: everybody
already had their friendship cliques, and none of them
were interested in bringing me into their fold. Two girls in
particular seemed to take pleasure in tormenting me: one
day they'd be nice as pie to me, acting as though I was a
member of their gang, and the next day they'd act like I
didn't exist, talking about me behind my back and making
me feel like a fool for ever having trusted them.

Throughout that year, I oscillated between feeling picked
on by the other students and feeling utterly isolated. Even
the teacher didn't seem interested in helping me to settle in.
One occasion in particular sticks in my mind: the teacher set
us a task for which we needed to work in groups, and said
that we could choose who we'd like to work with. One by
one, I watched all of the other children partnering up, and I
felt a sinking feeling in my stomach as I realised that nobody
was going to pick me.

"Miss," I said, as timidly as a mouse, "I'm not sure who I
should work with."

Barely taking the time to look me in the eye, the teacher
handed me a worksheet. "Here's a picture." She said,

brusquely, "just colour it in."

The teacher walked away before I had the chance to reply, so I sat and coloured in my picture, feeling totally alone.

Alone again, I overheard some of the kids whispering, from across the room. *She's alone again.* But none of them wanted to involve me. Nobody wanted to help.

That year, it was as though my whole personality changed. The instability of my home life, combined with the toxic environment of school, turned me into a shell of the person I had once been: I lost all of my confidence and became known as 'the shy one'. I felt as though I was totally lost, and it would take me many years - and many hard knocks - before I found myself again.

Virgin Mary socks

2

SCHOOL DAYS

First day at Eastwood Comprehensive

Luckily, I didn't have to stay at Lyncroft for long. Less than a year after starting there, it was time to move on to secondary school. When I arrived at Eastwood Comprehensive School on that first day of Year 7, I was really nervous. I was even more nervous when I saw the other new starters arriving with their primary school pals. *I'm the only one that's on her own,* I thought to myself, as I saw the Lyncroft girls arriving, arm in arm and laughing uproariously.

I may not have any friends yet, I told myself, as I walked alone through the school gates, *but at least I'm coming to school. Who knows, it may even be a fresh start.*

Luckily, I did make some friends at Eastwood Comprehensive. On the first day, I met a girl called Elisabeth. Elisabeth was a year older than me but had been held back a year, since she struggled to pay attention. She was always gazing dreamily out of the window during lessons, and forgetting to listen to what the teacher was saying. Nevertheless, we got on well enough: we both knew how it could feel to be the odd one out.

Another person that I met on that first day was a boy called William. William's surname began with B too, so we were both seated next to each other on the front row for the majority of our lessons. Little did we know, we would be sitting together for five years! Luckily, William was easy to get on with, and we worked together quite happily for the duration of our school careers. It made quite a difference to Lyncroft, where I'd so often felt that nobody wanted to work with me.

My closest friend from school though - and with whom I remain good friends to this day - was Claire. Claire - or Smedders as I call her - had to have a couple of months off of school due to an operation. When she returned, I noticed that the other girls had started leaving Claire out of their conversations. Having been through the same thing in primary school, I could empathise with Claire: the last thing that I wanted was for her to feel as isolated as I once had. With that in mind, I invited Claire to come and sit with William and me.

"How have you been?" I asked her, cheerfully. "How was your operation?"

Every morning from that day on, Claire would pull up a chair and sit with William and me. We would chat about this and that, or work together on whatever task the teacher had set, and neither of us had to worry about being left out by the other girls again. So began a friendship which has lasted until this day between Smedders and me.

As well as the few friends I had among the students, I tended to get on really well with the teachers too. There was Mrs Pearsey, my form tutor, who always seemed to be on the go, bustling around the classroom doing this and that, like the Duracell Bunny. There was Mrs Goldie, Mr Pickford and Miss Cooper, all of whom were supportive and kind. Mr Hepworth, my History teacher, didn't seem to be particularly fond of me: he characterised me as a bit of a dreamer, who stared out of the window rather than paying attention to his lessons. The thing was, I actually loved History! In fact, I still do. I love thinking about the history of places, in particular: the listed buildings and the ways they've been regenerated; the impact of war on the landscapes of towns; the stories trees could tell, if only they could speak. To Mr Hepworth, I may have looked as though I were daydreaming, but I was actually hanging on to his every word.

My favourite teacher by miles, though, was Mr Mavers. Mr Mavers was my Religious Education teacher in Year 7 and Year 8, and I absolutely loved him. I was his favourite student, and he always took the time to make me feel valued. I remember on one occasion, I walked past Mr Mavers' classroom while he was working on a project, and he invited me to come and be a part of filming it. Always happy to help Mr Manvers, I did so without question. Half an hour later, I was sitting in a French Lesson when Mr Mavers came by and knocked on the classroom door.

"I've just got something I wanted to drop off for Denise." He told my French teacher. "Thanks for all of your help today, Denise!" He said, warmly, presenting me with a Creme Egg he'd purchased from the school tuck shop.

Needless to say, all of the other students were extremely jealous of my Creme Egg! More importantly though, it was a little act of kindness that really stuck with me. In Year 9, we moved into a different part of the school with Mr Mavers, so he never taught me again, and I was devastated. I never forgot him though, and I'll always be grateful to him for the kindness and support he showed me in those early years of secondary school. Wherever he is now in the world, I wish him only the best.

***

Another teacher I was grateful to have in those early years of secondary school was my private tutor, Sister Celine. Sister Celine was, as you may have guessed, a nun. My Granny was a staunch Catholic and, seeing as she was keen on me having my first holy communion, she got me involved in the church. That was where I met Sister Celine, who noticed that I was a bit behind in English and Maths and offered to help me out.

From then on, every other Saturday from 10am to 12pm, I would head over to the Hilltop Catholic Church for lessons with Sister Celine. I felt a little bit embarrassed by it - I was very aware that the books I was reading were designed for children much younger than me - but the nuns were absolutely lovely to me. They'd always make a fuss over feeding me a big breakfast, despite the fact that I'd already eaten breakfast at home, and there was a grand piano which one of the nuns would always be playing whenever I visited. In fact, my fascination with their piano playing led them to recognise my passion for music: they were the first people that ever did.

I spent two years having sessions with Sister Celine, and I learned a lot in that short time. Gradually, as I became increasingly aware of my sexuality, I pulled away from the Catholic church and my attachment to it. Nevertheless, I'll always be grateful for my time with the nuns, and the faith they had in me.

***

I was in Year 9 when I had my first fight. Incidentally, it was my last fight too, but I have to admit: it was quite a dramatic one.

My opponent was a girl called Ellen. Ellen was always getting into fights with all kinds of people. In fact, I'd been feeling sorry for her about it. *When will people give this poor girl a break?* I asked myself. The next day, she started on me.

I was standing in the year room at the time. The year room was the place that our year group was allowed to spend our breaks when it was too rainy to go outside, and there was an office in the middle, where the Head of Year (ours, at the time, was Mr Pickford) was based, just in case anything 'kicked off'.

"I hear you've been calling me." Ellen said to me, one day, with a voice which told me she meant business.

"No I haven't-" I began to say, but I didn't have a chance to finish my sentence.

Before I could, Ellen had slapped me round the face!

That was it: I saw red. The next thing I knew, I was launching at Ellen and getting her into a headlock. Ellen tried to fight back. Blurry as the memory is, I remember her flailing around, limbs flying everywhere, trying to kick me but upending the bin instead.

"Fight! Fight! Fight!" The other kids in our year group chanted, delighted with the drama unfolding before their eyes.

Somehow, in the midst of all the adrenaline flooding through my system, I managed to remember some of the judo moves that my dad had taught me. See, what Ellen didn't know - in fact, none of the other kids at my school knew - was that my dad was a professional Judo player, and had been informally teaching me the art of self defence since I was a toddler. I can't quite believe that I found the presence of mind to use what he'd taught me, but I did: I summoned all my strength, pulled Ellen over my shoulder and slammed her down onto the ground.

Not long after, much to the dismay of the other students, Mr Pickford and Mrs Goldie appeared and broke up the fight. I was shaking as they pulled us apart.

"I didn't know you could fight." Somebody said to me, as I was taken away to the teacher's office.

"That isn't fighting," I said, "it's self-defense."

In the teacher's office, I assumed I was destined for a stack of detentions. To my surprise, that turned out to be far from the truth.

"Well, don't do it again." Mr Pickford said, after I'd finished explaining my version of events.

"But I didn't mean to do it the first time!" I protested.

"Well…" Mr Pickford replied, "*try* not to do it again!"

I was pretty confused to be getting off so lightly. "What?" I said. "Won't I be given a detention?"

Mr Pickford and Mrs Goldie exchanged knowing glances, before Mrs Goldie leaned forward and said, conspiratorially: "No, you won't. We saw what happened. You're not in trouble. In fact, you did well!"

With that, I was sent out of the office and the whole ordeal was over. Ellen was given a detention and I was let off scot-free. It had been an emotional and quite frightening experience, but at least I knew that no one would mess with me again. There was just one final bit of business to attend to, but it had to wait until that evening, when I got home and called Dad.

"Dad," I said into the receiver, hardly able to contain my excitement. "Dad! I did a JUDO MOVE!"

My Dad, Michael, my brother Martin, and myself

3

A DARK CHAPTER

After Mum and Dad separated, Mum remarried another man. I've suffered through a fair few struggles in my life so far, but I can confidently say that the five years we spent living with my mum's second husband were the worst five years of my life.

A lovely picture of me and my brother, but we're not happy due to our mum's marriage to a monster

From the age of ten to fifteen, my life was a living hell. The man in question brought so much misery to my life - and the life of my little brother, who was only four at the beginning - that I don't want to give him the dignity of naming him in this book. In the anecdotes that follow, I'll refer to him simply as 'him'.

In short, he was an angry man. He would lose his temper unexpectedly and without warning, and when he lost his temper, he became violent. When he became violent, I became his favourite target.

On one occasion, I came home from school and discovered that Mum was still at work. He was home though, watching television in the living room.

"Have you got any homework?" He asked me, in his typically gruff way.

"Yes." I replied. "I'll go to my bedroom and do it." I had no interest in spending any more time around him than I absolutely had to.

That evening, I had plans to go and hang out with friends, so I was quite happy to head up to my room and get my homework out of the way. I shut the door behind me, popped the radio on and settled down to get on with my work in peace.

But the peace didn't last long. Suddenly, he was barging into my room, clearly full of his characteristic venom. He didn't so much as knock.

"That music's a bit loud!" He snarled at me. "I want you

to turn it down."

"Sorry, I didn't realise." I said, standing up to turn the radio off. I already knew though, in my heart, that it was too late. When he was angry like this, there was no hope of reasoning with him.

"You never listen to me!" He continued, his voice thick with rage.

"What?!" I asked, genuinely perplexed. After all, I had already stood up in order to turn the music down.

"I can't hear myself think!" He yelled, reflexively clenching and unclenching his fists. "I'm going to teach you a lesson."

At the time, we lived across the road from a video shop which - if we were lucky - would let my friends and me take home some of their old posters, once they'd finished with them. I had a big *Sister Act* pinned to the back of my door, and it was my pride and joy. I also had a few music posters dotted around the walls too: Peter Andre; the Spice Girls... Before I had a chance to even respond to his threat, he was tearing my beloved posters down from the wall, one by one. The next thing I knew, it was me that he was lunging for.

He grabbed me by the hair and tugged me so close to him that I could feel his hot breath on my face.

"Never do this again." He spat.

What did I even do to make him so angry?! I asked myself, though I wouldn't have dared to say so out loud. Who knows what he would have done if I'd dared to defy him.

He tugged my hair again: this time with such force that he tore the skin of my scalp - a scar which I bear to this day, as a daily reminder of his vicious cruelty.

Later, when Mum was home, I told her everything. She looked at my tear streaked face; she looked at my tattered posters; she looked at his calm, placid face.

"Your daughter was going mad." He told her, coolly. "I just left her to it."

Eventually, devastatingly, Mum sided with him. He was an adult, after all, and he was a seasoned liar. He always seemed to have an excuse: 'She's been in a fight at school.' He'd say. 'She's been fighting with her little brother again.' I always wondered how he could lose his temper so easily with me, but stay so calm when he was lying about it afterwards.

Whatever the excuse, Mum always seemed to believe him.

"Why do you always have to play up for him?" She'd ask me. "Why do you have to be such a cow to him?"

And then, to add insult to injury, Mum hit me too.

On another occasion, he wasn't so lucky.

This time, I was sitting in the living room with Rocky - the dog that we had after Lady died - and Martin. We were just watching the television and minding our own business when we heard a strange banging sound coming from upstairs.

"I'll go and see what it is, Martin. You wait here." I told my little brother.

As I headed up the stairs to find out what the banging

noise was all about, I saw him standing at the stop of the staircase. The way that he stood seemed to block out all of the light; it was as though his presence was shrouding the house in eerie darkness.

"What's going on?" I began to say, before noticing a lightbulb on the floor.

Thinking that he might have dropped the bulb, I crouched down to pick it up, but the glass was so hot that it scalded my hand.

"Ow!" I exclaimed, reflexively, and as I released the bulb from my grasp, I felt his hands upon me again.

Suddenly, the house was in chaos. He had grabbed me by the hair and was tugging me violently to and fro, while I fought with all my might to get away from him. From the bottom of the stairs, Martin screamed and Rocky barked, both of them pleading in their own way for him to let me go.

Suddenly, above all the chaos, there was the voice of my mother.

"GET YOUR HANDS OFF OF MY DAUGHTER!" She yelled.

He let me go. In the seconds that followed, the house fell into a strange silence, and Martin and I were sent to our rooms.

Soon, the house was full of chaos again, but this time it was Mum and him. They screamed at one another for what felt like hours. *Maybe this is it.* I thought to myself. *Now, at last, she knows that I'm not lying. She knows that he's the problem.*

Maybe now she'll kick him out for good.

But it was a hopeless dream. Mum forgave him, and it wasn't long before the attacks continued.

Over the course of those five years, his attacks on me were relentless. In the course of an average week, he would lay his hands on me multiple times. My only relief was when I stayed with my dad or my granny, or when I had a sleepover at a friend's house. He once made the mistake of attacking me in front of my cousin Lisa, and all hell broke loose.

Lisa and I had decided to make chocolate crispy cakes, and had headed to the Co-op in Eastwood in order to get the ingredients. Upon our return, we did make a bit of a mess of the kitchen, though we'd promised him that we would clear it up. After all, it was only a harmless bit of mess: we were just two teenage girls spending our Friday evening making cakes.

But two teenagers having some harmless fun wasn't acceptable to him. When he saw the mess we'd made, he smacked me. Hard. Lisa wasted no time in grabbing my arm and bundling me out of the house. Before I knew it, we were in a phonebox calling Lisa's mum. Lisa's mum was livid, and she called Dad and my auntie Karen.

"Stay where you are." Auntie Karen warned. "We're coming to get you."

So we did just that. We waited, nervously, in the telephone box until the adults arrived. Dad was seething with rage, and took us straight back to the house to confront my abuser.

"You've just attacked my daughter!" He yelled. "And for what?! Making some mess with some chocolate cake?! You've got no right to lay your hands on my daughter."

Suddenly, he didn't look like such a big and scary man, with my dad screaming in his face. I went home with Dad that night and slept at his house. It was a huge relief to be away from the nightmarish reality of my home.

But I couldn't avoid him forever. I always had to go home eventually. And he'd always find ways to get to me, especially when Mum wasn't around.

In fact, over the course of those dozens and dozens of attacks, there was only one other occasion when Mum saw. We were sitting in the living room as a family, watching the television. I was sitting on the floor near his chair, with a glass of pop in my hand. I was about to take a sip of my drink when Rocky the dog walked past and gave me an affectionate lick to the face, as he was wont to do.

"CRACK!"

Suddenly, out of the blue, I felt a huge smack on the back of my head.

"You made Rocky do that!" He snarled.

Mum was in the room and - while she did scold him a little bit for raising a hand to me - she didn't say much. I wonder if that's why - out of all of the attacks over the years - this is one of the few that I remember clearly. I think I'd often dreamed of the moment when Mum would witness his behaviour. *Maybe then,* I told myself, *it'll finally stop.* But now she had seen, and it still hadn't stopped. Maybe that memory stays with me because it was the day that I gave up hope.

But finally, at long last, it did stop.

I was fifteen years old and arriving home from school when I saw the car parked outside the house. Its boot was wide open, which caught my attention. I quickly realised that there were, in fact, two cars, and his mother was piling boxes into one of them.

"Hello, are you alright?" I asked her, puzzled. "What's going on?"

She simply grunted in response. She'd never been a particularly friendly woman, but on that day, she was even colder. Luckily though, I didn't need to wait long for an answer to my question. A few moments later, he emerged from the house, his arms laden with boxes, my mum following behind him with a suitcase.

"He's been having an affair." Mum said, matter of factly. "So now he's moving out."

His affair was with the sister of a girl in my class at school. She'd just turned eighteen, and this wasn't the first time he'd been involved with her. He'd cheated on my mum with her two years earlier, when he was twenty nine and she was only sixteen. When Mum found out, the girl had left town and Mum had forgiven him. Now, the girl was back again, and Mum wasn't going to be fooled twice.

"I'll have that wedding ring back." He said, after shoving

the last of his boxes into the boot of his car.

Mum wasted no time in honouring his request. Without hesitation, she pulled the ring off of her finger and hurled it into the grass verge.

"You can have your bastard wedding ring back!" She told him cheerfully, and turned back towards the house.

Way to go, Mum, I thought to myself, as we headed back inside. *If only you'd done this the first time he cheated, you might have saved Martin and me from two years of abuse.*

I've had a lot of happy moments in my life, but still none of them have topped that day. September 11th 1997: the day that my abuser left, and my hellish house became a home again.

***

He may have been gone from my house from that day, but it took a while to shake off the damage he'd done. For some time, I felt as though I was anticipating his return. *Will Mum forgive him?* I kept asking myself. *Will he turn up and lay his hands on me again?* Luckily, he never did come back, and gradually, I was able to heal.

He stayed with that girl for some time: long enough for them to get engaged, before she lost interest and left him for somebody else. That engagement gave Mum a good opportunity to get her own back, though. We weren't invited, of course. However, with the help of a few friends,

Mum made sure that the party was peppered with surprises. First of all, she called in a party sized order from just about every local takeaway, and had it delivered to his address. Even better, she arranged for a troupe of strippers to pay a visit. By all accounts, they arrived dressed in police uniforms, so he let them in , thinking he might be in some kind of trouble. Since I was at home, watching with glee as the staff of our local Chinese takeaway piled trays and trays of takeaway into their delivery car, I'll never know for sure what happened with those strippers. From what I heard though, the look on his face was priceless as they conducted a 'strip search' of the party hosts!

4

A LIFE CHANGING DIAGNOSIS

When I was in my very early twenties, I was away on a caravan holiday in a place called Ingoldmells, near Lincolnshire. There was a big group of us: Mum, Amanda, a cousin, his girlfriend, some friends and my auntie Karen. We were having a lovely time and all getting on well. However, one evening, Auntie Karen started a conversation with Mum which would change the course of my life.

"There's something not right about Denise." She said to Mum.

"What do you mean?" Mum asked.

"I'm not exactly sure what I mean." Auntie Karen said. "It's just something I've noticed. The way she does her chores so slowly... I'm not trying to worry you. But I wonder if you should go to a doctor."

As soon as we were back from our holiday, we did just that. Mum and Dad got together and agreed that I should go to the QMC. When we arrived for our appointment, I talked to the doctor and did a few tests. Surprisingly, I was given a diagnosis straight away.

"You've got a mild global learning disability." The doctor explained.

The news took a while to sink in. I was embarrassed. Did this mean that people would think I was some kind of freak? Did it mean that they would look at me differently from now on?

Gradually, though, the doctor's diagnosis started to make sense. Now, I understood why I had always been in the bottom set at school. I understood why it had always taken me longer than the other kids to learn things. Ultimately, I came to realise, the diagnosis didn't change anything about who I was. This global learning disability was something I'd already been living with and coping with for my entire life. Now, at least, I had a name for it. I could accept that this was simply a part of who I was. I wasn't and still am not thick: I'm simply me; unique and perfectly made, exactly as I am. It reminds me of the lyrics to a famous song by Lady Gaga, which perfectly encapsulate how I feel about my diagnosis:

"Don't hide yourself in regret, just love yourself and you're set. I'm on the right track, baby, I was born this way!"

5

MUSIC AND ME

An 80s Christmas night in my Christmas hoodie

John came up with my stage name and supported me

All my life, I've loved music.

I was nine years old when I wrote my first song, when I was still at Granby Junior School. I wasn't much of a fan of pen and paper, but as I.C.T. began to be incorporated into our education, I found the freedom of the keyboard liberating, and I started writing songs on the computer instead of by hand.

My creativity slowed down a bit while I was struggling at school. Perhaps the troubles I faced with friendships dulled my spark a little bit. Luckily, I found it again: when I was fifteen, my creativity came flowing back, and I couldn't seem to stop writing music.

Aged 23 or 24 - I was having a photoshoot for one of my tracks

When I was nineteen, I began a two year Music course at Clarendon College. Put simply, I absolutely loved it. After a bad start at another college - with a Dance tutor who seemed more intent on humiliating me than educating me - I had my doubts about the course at Clarendon. In the end though, the two environments couldn't have been more different. At Clarendon, I was far away from everyone I knew in Ilkeston and Eastwood. It was a fresh start with all kinds of new people, and - after a long period of feeling ostracised by and isolated from my peers - I finally felt I could just be myself.

We did all kinds of things at Clarendon College. We sang; we participated in bands; we played instruments; we regularly performed on stage. One of the most exciting things that we got to do, though, was visiting local schools to perform for their students. A particular school visit stands out in my mind as a memory I'll cherish forever. We visited Matthew Holland School to perform for their students, and I had the opportunity to sing on stage. I'm not sure what was in the water at Matthew Holland School, but the kids in the audience were absolutely wild. They couldn't seem to get enough of our performances, and were screaming and cheering as though they were at Glastonbury.

Their enthusiasm certainly fed into the confidence of our performance; when it was my turn to sing, I took the microphone and decided to experiment with a bit of audience interaction.

"Now, it's my turn to give you a song, but I need your

help!" I declared, into the crowd of children, who seemed barely able to contain their excitement. "Who would like to come up on the stage for five minutes of fame?!"

In response to this question, the students seemed to erupt into a whole new level of chaos and commotion. Dozens of hands shot up into the air, and a chorus of "Me! Me! Me!" emerged from every corner of the assembly hall.

"But hang on," I added, thoroughly enjoying the experience of a room full of elated children hanging on my every word, "what about your teachers?! Could you pick a teacher for me, and send them up to the stage?!"

This request was met with squeals of delight from all over the room. Eventually, a teacher was chosen: an Irish man by the name of Mr Egan was ferried onto the stage, looking slightly overwhelmed. All I can say is - Mr Egan, if you're reading this: I'm sorry. I sat the poor fella on a chair in the centre of the stage and proceeded to perform a particularly raunchy rendition of Madonna's 'Don't Tell Me'. By the time I sat on Mr Egan's knee, the kids were practically rioting, standing on their chairs and clapping so loudly that it felt as though the roof might fall in. Poor Mr Egan's face turned about as pink as my cowboy hat, which I threw into the delighted crowd. What can I say? I was enjoying my moment in the limelight!

As we were preparing to leave, one of the sound engineers approached me with a knowing smirk on his face.

"Do you know who he is?" He asked me, hardly containing his glee.

"Who, Mr Egan?" I asked, utterly puzzled.

"Yeah. Do you know who his brother is?"

"No... How would I know anything about him?!"

"Well, you're not going to believe this, but the headteacher just told me. Mr Egan is Kian Egan's brother... Kian from Westlife!"

It was the icing on the cake after what had already been a riot of a day. Not only had I performed to the most enthusiastic bunch of students I'd ever come across, I'd got a new claim to fame: making Kian from Westlife's brother blush by sitting on his knee!

**

Another treasured memory in my musical journey was my foray into karaoke, which began about ten years ago. There was a karaoke night being run on Sundays at a pub called The Borough (now The Lounge) in Ilkeston. I decided to go along and - upon finding out that there was a karaoke competition taking place - I decided to sign myself up. I'd never been in a competition until that day, but I figured I had nothing to lose. The organisers told me that I had to pick two songs, so I picked Alexandra Burke's version of 'Hallelujah' and 'The Edge of Glory' by Lady Gaga.

Considering it was a Sunday night, the pub was absolutely heaving. It seemed as though the whole of Ilkeston had turned up, so there was a fair bit of pressure! My rendition of Hallelujah went well enough, but it's a slow and romantic number, and I felt as though I needed to up the energy. So, for the second song, I decided that I had to go all out. I snuck into the toilets and changed into a full Lady Gaga costume: I had the outfit, the wig... You name it! Well, that costume gave me the confidence I needed to deliver an amazing performance.

Me, as Lady Gaga, winning a karaoke competition

I took control of the stage that night in a way I hadn't done since that Madonna performance with Mr Egan. It was such a buzz, and the crowd seemed to absolutely love it. Even better, of the twelve contestants (one of whom was my ex-girlfriend - no pressure there...), the panel of judges declared me the winner! I was elated as I stepped to the front to collect my prize - a bottle of champagne and £100. I'd put my heart and soul into my performance, and it felt great to have that recognised.

After that, I rediscovered my love of the stage, and I began performing locally more often. I also decided to take my own original music more seriously. I recorded two of my own songs - 'VIP', about the experience of being on a night out and receiving 5* treatment, and 'Broken Silence', about a homophobic attack I once faced. My music is available on both Spotify and Apple Music. In 2021, my songs were streamed 52,700 times. I can't put into words the sense of pride and achievement that I feel, knowing that my music has reached so many people. What's more, if even one person reading this book feels inspired to put their own creative efforts out there, after hearing my story, I'll be a happy woman indeed.

The Day I Met The Vengaboys!

I designed my own hoodie and trousers, but the Vengaboys gave me this hat!

Open-top bus with Smedders on a day trip to Ingoldmells

Me, Brett, and Smedders - having a good night

6

COMING OUT

In my early teens, I didn't really think much about romance. I suppose I was too consumed by the conflict at home to have much interest in relationships.

But then, when I was seventeen, I met a dance teacher at college, and I realised that I had feelings for her.

For a while, I kept my feelings to myself. Throughout my childhood and in my early teens - both at school and at home - I'd had plenty of experience of being an outsider. I didn't feel particularly accepted at college anyway, so coming out seemed like too big a risk to take. I just didn't believe that I'd be accepted if I revealed who I really was.

It was only when I got to Clarendon College, where I met a tribe of likeminded people who accepted me exactly as I was, with all of my quirks and eccentricities, that I finally felt able to speak the truth about my identity.

My cousin Emma was the first person that I told. Feeling more than a little bit anxious, I knocked on for Emma at her house.

"Can we go for a walk?" I asked.

"Sure," Emma said, grabbing her coat. "What's up?"

I waited until we'd been out for a while before I summoned the courage to speak. We were sitting on a pavement, and I could feel my heart pounding in my chest.

"Emma, I've got something to tell you." I said. "And I'm really nervous."

"There's no need to worry." Emma responded, giving me a reassuring smile. "Whatever it is, I'll support you."

I told Emma that I was bisexual. I knew, even then, that it wasn't the full truth: I had no interest in men, and I never had. But at the time, it was the easier thing to say, and I was relieved to have said it to someone that I could trust.

True to her word, Emma did support me. Now that I'd confided in her, it didn't seem quite so scary to confide in other people too. Bit by bit, as I felt ready to, I started to tell other people. I told people from college and friends first, before gradually telling people in my family too. It wasn't until I was twenty one that I started telling people the whole truth: that I was a lesbian. But eventually, I got there.

Mum said that she'd known since I was fourteen. I was surprised to hear it, seeing as I certainly hadn't known myself when I was fourteen, but I suppose that - sometimes - our family do know us better than we know ourselves.

The very last person to know was my granny. Granny was a Catholic, and a very traditional woman, so I knew that she'd struggle to accept the truth. Nevertheless, I loved

Granny and needed to know that she could love and accept me exactly as I was. I knew that - eventually - I needed to tell her.

The right moment finally came, strangely enough, on a random Wednesday, following a particularly heavy night of drinking: for me, not Granny. I had been to a pub called The Roundhouse with Amanda and another friend of ours, Steven. The three of us used to enjoy going to an alternative music night on Tuesdays, and - on this particular occasion - I'd managed to put away a quite impressive number of Reefs.

Afterwards, I headed back to Granny's, since I was staying with her at the time. As I got through the front door, I realised that all of the lights in the house were off.

Granny must be fast asleep. I thought for myself, as I wrestled off my shoes. *I'd better be really quiet and go straight to bed.*

But - of course - people that have had one too many bottles of Reef aren't particularly good at sneaking quietly to bed. Within a few moments, and with an enormous crashing sound, I found myself tangled up in Granny's stairlift at the bottom of the stairs.

Immediately, a light pinged on, and poor Granny headed downstairs to help me up to my bedroom. It was only once I was with Granny, struggling to get up the stairs, that I realised quite how drunk I was. I had to be propped up against the wall, where I leaned against the lightswitch, causing it to repeatedly switch off and on again.

"Granny!" I said, pointing at the flickering light, oblivious to the fact that I was the one causing the flickering. "I think you've got a ghost!"

The next morning, Granny had a few stern words for me about coming home in such a state. I apologised, but Granny wasn't going to let me get off that lightly.

"Who were you out with exactly?" She probed.

When I mentioned Steven's name, she tutted.

"See, out with men and in that state. Anything could've happened to you. Men take advantage of girls in that state."

I gently reassured Granny that she had absolutely nothing to worry about, but the lecture continued. Repeatedly, I tried to let her know that there was no chance of me getting carried away or caught up in the moment with any of the men I went drinking with, but Granny wasn't taking the hint.

Eventually, I decided to spell it out.

"Granny," I said, taking a deep breath to settle my nerves. "I'm just going to tell you. I - don't - fancy - men."

As soon as I'd said the words, I stood up and left the room. Frankly, I was terrified of seeing how Granny would react, and I couldn't bear to stay long enough to find out. So, before she had a chance to say anything, I left the house.

Later that day, when I sheepishly returned to Granny's house. She wouldn't talk to me. It was exactly as I'd expected: she was a traditional, religious woman and she was worried about me. I was determined to make my peace with Granny, though.

"Look, Granny," I said to her. "I know it isn't a phase. I know myself, and I know how I feel most comfortable. I just want to be able to talk to you truthfully about my life, and about who I am. I don't want to have to hide the truth from you."

It took a while, but Granny did come around. A few days later, she spoke to me again.

"I want you to be able to talk to me about the truth, too." She told me. "I love you for who you are."

When Granny passed away in 2005, it was a huge source of comfort to me that I had been able to speak the truth to her, and that she had responded with acceptance and love.

After having felt so isolated at school, and always being made to feel like the 'odd one out', I feel immensely proud of the fact that I have not only embraced my true identity but have become an ally for the LGBT+ community. Over the years I've attended pride marches in Derby, Nottingham, Birmingham, Manchester and even Benidorm! Mum even came with me to the Benidorm one: she had a great time! We joined the march along the seafront before heading to a gay bar called Sensations; the owners - Marco and Sammy - are two of the nicest and most welcoming guys that you could ever hope to meet. They make me feel like family whenever I go back there. I always make sure to have a drink with Sammy when I do, particularly since he considers it an offence on a par with swearing if you turn down his offer of a shot!

My first ever rainbow t-shirt

To me, it's very fitting that the pride flag is a rainbow, but because being embraced by the LGBT+ community really has injected my life with so much more colour and joy. I feel as though my world has opened up, and I've found 'my people'. My best friend Brett is gay too: we met seventeen years ago, in a pub called The Warren in Ilkeston. I'd gone there with Mum and her partner, Valdo, when they told me that there was somebody they'd like me to meet.

That somebody was Brett, and we hit it off then and there. Seventeen years later, we're still the best of friends. I wouldn't change a thing about him. It's great to have a best friend who knows what it's like to be gay, and how that can sometimes make you feel like an outsider. It can be really difficult accepting your sexuality, and having people who understand that struggle and make you feel seen is important. For that reason, I'm currently mentoring two teenage girls who are currently working through the process of 'coming out' themselves. For me, it's very rewarding to help young LGBT+ people to embrace their identity, by being an older role model and showing them that they're not alone.

My partner in crime, bitch!

Having a male best friend means that people often mistake Brett and me for a couple. Sometimes, it's just easier to let them believe it! In reality though, I am currently single. I'm a romantic at heart and would very much like to fall in love and settle down. However, as much as I would like to find love, I'm holding out for the right person. I don't intend to settle until I've found someone truly special.

Me and my Miss J (Jackie)

7
BREAKING DOWN

There's a famous saying that 'it's always darkest before the dawn'. I discovered the truth in this phrase in my mid twenties, when a series of tragic events led me to my own version of rock bottom. It was a dark time, from which it took me many years to find the light again.

Things started to go downhill when I lost my Nana Mary, on the 20th July 2004. Nana was diagnosed with cancer in March of that year, and was told that she'd live until Christmas. This terminal diagnosis was difficult enough to make sense of, but losing her in the summer made it even more of a shock. Nana's death was my first experience of losing a loved one, and it hit me hard. When I went to see her in her coffin, it was my first time seeing a person that has passed: it didn't feel real, and seeing her like that, wearing a bandana to conceal her loss of hair, and looking so frail and fragile, was a real shock to the system.

A year later, I lost my Granny too. Granny Rose passed away on September 23rd 2005, having contracted pneumonia during a hospital stay. In some ways, I was still grieving Nana's passing, and losing Granny Rose - who had been one of the most important figures in my life, and was more like a parent than a grandparent - hit me like a ton of bricks. It was then that I really began to lose a grip of my mental health.

For some reason, I felt compelled to get out of the country. I moved to Benidorm and didn't return for six months, thinking that a change of scenery and the warmer weather might help me to find some inner peace. It didn't work. When I returned, I felt just as unstable, but I had the added problem of having no home to go to. I stayed at a friend's flat for a whole, but the friend soon started to make me feel uncomfortable, following me around whenever I went out and making me feel unsafe. I started to sofa surf, all the while feeling less and less secure. I was grieving, I was lonely and I had nowhere to call home. It was the perfect recipe for a breakdown.

In June 2010, when I was twenty eight, I was provided with a place to stay by a mental health charity organisation in Ilkeston. My new address was 1 Stanhope Street - a four bedroom house with a shared bathroom, kitchen and living space. It was a lovely house with friendly people, and it should have marked the beginning of my getting better. Unfortunately, however, the staff tasked with supporting me and my new housemates were seemingly intent on making my life a living hell.

My support worker, who I'll call J, was nice enough at first. It was after Christmas that things started to change, and it felt as though J had turned against me.

At the time, I paid a service charge - a chunk of my jobseekers allowance which covered my bills in the house on Stanhope Street. I paid £22 a fortnight, and J would drop by the house to collect it from me. I always thought it was a little strange that the money wasn't taken directly from my benefits, but I appreciated that it was a fair amount for the house I was living in, so I didn't complain. I just put the money into a brown envelope and waited at home when J came to collect it.

One day though, shortly after Christmas, things were different. I was having a pyjama day, relaxing on the sofa and watching some rubbish on the telly. All of a sudden, J barged in.

"Hello, are you alright?" I asked, struggling to keep the note of concern from my voice. It was clear from the moment she entered the room that things weren't alright.

"I'm glad you're here," she responded, seemingly with no time for a friendly hello. "It was you I wanted to see."

It was at this point that I noticed that J was holding a letter with an envelope.

"What's going on?" I asked.

"You need to give us more money."

"What?"

"You need to give us more money." J repeated. "We've

paid something to the council and you have to pay us back."

"How much?" I asked, feeling quite concerned. My jobseekers benefits didn't exactly leave me rolling in spare cash.

"£50 a week."

"£50 a week?!" I could hardly believe what I was hearing. "What's it for?!"

But J wouldn't tell me. All she would tell me is that if I didn't pay, I'd be 'out on my ear'. I felt vulnerable, betrayed and attacked. I felt as though J was trying to take advantage of me, which stung: after all, I'd hit rock bottom and was just starting to feel as though I could get back on my feet, and now I was being manipulated by the person I was supposed to be relying on for help. As J left, she flippantly commented that I should be able to use my disability allowance to pay the money. To me, that comment hurt. It felt as though J thought that my disability money was something I could afford to throw around without thinking about it. It was as though she didn't think I needed it at all.

On another occasion, J told me that she'd be coming to collect my money at 9.30am that Wednesday.

"That's fine." I told her. "But just so you know, I'll be going into Nottingham later on that morning. I'm meeting my friend Smedders, and I have to set off at 11am."

J agreed. When 9.30am on Wednesday arrived, I was ready. I'd been to the shop and got out my money, and was waiting on the sofa with my envelope. But J was nowhere to be seen.

At 10am, Smedders rang.

"Just stick with the plan." I told her. "If she's still not here, just get the bus as planned. I told her where I was going. If she's not here, she's not here."

At about 10.30am, I called the office. J wasn't there. *What can I do?* I thought. *I've tried my best.* I popped the envelope in my bag and headed into town to meet Smedders.

When we got to town, Smedders and I - thinking that we'd like to get some food before we started shopping - went to a pub called Squares. We'd just ordered food when my phone started ringing. What do you know: it was J.

"Where are you?" She demanded.

"I'm in Nottingham, getting something to eat." I replied, trying to keep my voice calm. "Where are you?"

"I'm at your house!" She snapped.

"Well, I told you I had to go out at 11am." I said.

"Well why didn't you leave the money in your bedroom?!"

"I'm not that stupid!" I said. "I can't just leave money lying around!" I could hear the anger in my voice now - I was struggling to stay calm, but what did she expect? I felt as though I was being harassed by a school bully rather than helped by my support worker.

"You need to come back right now!"

"Well, I'm not! I'll come back when I come back, and I'll drop the money off at the office when I do."

This back and forth carried on for a while, becoming more and more heated, until I found myself losing my composure completely. I hurled a stream of expletives at J and hung up on her, before turning my phone off completely.

From that point on, things never really recovered between J and me. She was supposed to be my support worker, but I was the last person that she wanted to help. When I found out that I wasn't allowed to leave the country while claiming disability allowance, and that I'd been reported for my trip to Benidorm, I turned to J for help.

"You know," she said, her voice as cold and hard as ice. "I don't actually think you have a disability."

I was too stunned to speak. *How dare you.* I thought to myself. *How dare you.* But I didn't say anything to J. Instead, I went home, cried and called dad. He managed to calm me down enough that I gained the confidence to deal with the issue myself, which I did. Nevertheless, I knew that I could never rely on J for support again.

Little incidents after that began to chip away more and more at my fragile sense of stability. When I used a heater in the living room, J confiscated it without telling me, claiming that it was a fire hazard to use it in a communal area. My birthday cards, apparently, were a fire hazard too, so J took them down from the mantelpiece without discussion.

Finally, shortly after my 29th birthday, J served me with a seven day eviction notice. On the seventh day, returning from an appointment, I found that my belongings - which had been packed and ready to go in my bedroom - had been unceremoniously dumped on the pavement outside the house. No discussions, no support, no compassion. *So much for charity,* I thought.

I never saw J again after that. I said my farewells to those at the charity that had supported me, and I moved on. Luckily, I had something else lined up with another charity. This charity was Deventio and - thank goodness - things were finally about to get better.

8

WORK

Derventio – the first Christmas decoration I made

Sometimes, when I think about the lower moments I've experienced in my life, it can be hard to believe how far I've come. One of the areas where that change feels sharpest is my work.

There have been times in my adult life where I have been unable to work. I've been homeless, unemployed and consumed by mental health challenges. At times like that, it can be hard to hold on to hope that there's light at the end of the tunnel; it can be hard to hold faith in the fact that things will get better. But for me, they have.

That low moment - following the breakdown which I have explained in the previous chapter - left me feeling that I had nowhere to turn. I had trusted the charity which J worked for, and that trust had left me vulnerable. When I moved on to another charity - the Derventio Housing Trust - I had big fears that I might face a similar situation. What if the staff at Derventio were just like J? What if I let my guard down with them, only to be hurt once more? Well, the saying goes that 'it's always darkest before the dawn': I didn't know it yet but - after the darkness that had dominated my late twenties - Derventio's arrival into my life marked the first glimmer of a new dawn.

The particular individual at Derventio to whom I am most grateful is Becky. I ended up spending five years living in the shared accommodation at Derventio and, in that time, Becky really took me under her wing. She got me involved in all kinds of volunteer work over the years: I did arts and crafts; I cooked; I even worked on a farm near Kirk Langley! Gradually, I began to recover the things that I had lost, and began to emerge from the darkness. After spending so much time outdoors in the countryside, I was starting to feel hopeful again. As a result of the valuable work I was doing, I was starting to feel purposeful again. And thanks to the connections I made with my new colleagues, I began to feel like part of a community again. Slowly but surely, I was remembering how good life could be.

While working at Derventio, I got involved with a project called 'Homeless Sunday' - a church event designed to raise awareness of the plight of homeless people. The event was to be held at Derbyshire Cathedral, and East Midlands Today were interested in interviewing some of the staff and volunteers. Jackie - the woman in charge of Homeless Sunday - asked me if I'd like to be involved. Seeing as I'd been close to homelessness myself in the past, it would be a good opportunity to share my experiences while raising the profile of the organisation at the same time.

At first, I was nervous being in front of the camera. I suppose I was a bit uncertain about what questions I might be asked in the interview. In the end though, I loved it. I suppose it may come as no surprise, following on from the Mr Egan story earlier in this book, but I do enjoy the limelight from time to time, particularly when I get to perform. I decided to read a poem, and ended up quite enjoying the process, even if the East Midlands Today crew weren't quite as rapturous as Mr Egan's students had been! Afterwards, I headed home to watch myself on the telly, and it seemed as though the majority of Ilkeston tuned in too. I got some great feedback about being such a natural in front of the camera, and my confidence soared as a result of having been involved in such a valuable project.

Derventio arts & crafts with Pip

One of my favourite people at Derventio was a volunteer coordinator called Helen. When Helen decided to move on, I was absolutely gutted: working with her had given me so much purpose and value, and I feared that Derventio might fall apart without her. On her final day, I gave Helen a card and included my contact details, hoping that she might stay in touch. A little while later, to my delight, she called me.

"Denise," she said, "when can you meet up? I want to discuss a new opportunity with you."

The opportunity in question was a chance to volunteer alongside Helen at her new place of work: Healthwatch Derbyshire. At around this point, I was moving out of my shared accommodation at Derventio, so I was in the right frame of mind for a fresh start at work, too. Plus, I was excited by the opportunity to work with Helen again. With that in mind, I took her up on her offer and got stuck in.

My first job with Healthwatch Derbyshire was just handing out leaflets. Gradually though, I moved towards more specialised work, shadowing staff in order to build my experience. Before long, I began visiting and inspecting care homes in the local area, alongside Derbyshire County Council, in order to make recommendations about how their grounds and accommodations could be improved. Being able to affect change and improve the lives of vulnerable people gave me an enormous sense of wellbeing, and I have never looked back from my decision to get involved with the organisation. I've even had the opportunity to get in front of the camera again: this year, we made a video for people with learning difficulties, encouraging them to attend their annual health checks. I had the chance to star in the video, so keep an eye out on YouTube over the next few months!

Recently, I attended an AGM for Healthwatch Derbyshire. It was held in Matlock and - clearly having tapped into my passion for performance - the organisers asked me to participate in a roleplay, in which I had to play a silly doctor. Again, I was nervous beforehand, and I only had less than twenty four hours to prepare. Nevertheless, I seemed to pull it out of the bag again, and made the audience laugh. What more can you ask for?!

In addition to the roleplay, I also have a small talk at the AGM, regarding my role at the organisation. In a way, this kind of 'performance' is more intimidating to me than the more creative kind, so I was really proud of myself for putting myself out there. Best of all though, my talk caught the eye of one of the women in the audience.

"My organisation is looking for people just like you!" She said, pulling me to one side after the event. "But they'll pay you for it!"

I'd been so happy with the fulfilment and purpose I'd gained from my work with Derventio and Healthcare Derbyshire, I'd never even contemplated an actual paid role. But somehow, here I was. The woman who had spoken to me at the AGM (who, it transpired, worked for an organisation called Inclusion North) got in touch with Helen, asking her to encourage me to apply. Helen helped me with the application form and, next thing I knew, she was accompanying me to an interview.

The interview was in Ripley, and there were three people on the panel - Ali, Sandy and Gary. All three of them worked for Inclusion North, but only Gary was an EBE. An EBE is an 'Expert by Experience': a person with lived experience of any of the key issues catered to by the organisation. This was my first proper job interview, and I was more than a little nervous, but what could I do except for my best? I turned up wearing a new outfit and a big smile, and made an effort to answer all of the interviewers' questions with thoughtfulness and honesty. Thankfully, it was enough. A few days later, I got a phone call from Sandy confirming that I'd got the job.

Three years later, I'm still working with Inclusion North, and I couldn't be more grateful for the opportunities and experiences I've had with the organisation. I've been involved with all sorts at Inclusion North: I work alongside a guy called Craig in producing the organisation's Covid 19 news for social media; I help to train new staff and volunteers; I'm a member of a monthly expert advisory group; I've done more role plays and even sat on interview panels! The main bulk of my work though is assisting in the production of Care and Treatment Reviews for people with Autism and learning disabilities. In practice, this entails going to hospitals from Derby to Chesterfield, meeting with people who have been doing 'long stays' in hospital and helping them to get back on their feet and live their lives with the right care in place. Like Gary, I am now an EBE, and my personal experience of living with a learning difficulty helps me to understand and support others in similar circumstances to get the best out of their lives.

Words can't describe how happy I am to be able to give back and support those in need, after I was the person in need for so long.

Being interviewed for the Jo Wiley Campaign for Disability Rights

EPILOGUE

What is life like now?

How I looked 10 years ago at the age of 29!

A more updated photo!

N ow that you've heard my story - the highs and the lows - I'd like to end by telling you where I am now. What are the things that fill my days now, and what are my hopes and dreams for the future?

Well, I'm happy to say that my life now is the best that it has ever been. I am a happy and confident person with a great network of friends, a fulfilling career and plenty of hobbies. I'm lucky enough to spend my time going to gigs, making music and hanging out with the people I love. What more could a person ask for?

Looking good on a night out

A family member from The Hillside in Ireland, Anne

Me, cousin Jackie Dad, Stepmum Sue, my friend Sue, Brett, Smedders, aunty Margaret, cousin Yvonne - afternoon tea for my birthday

My mind is always buzzing with new ideas for the future. One of the next things on my agenda is to create a unisex perfume. I'd like to keep making more music, too. Also, as soon as this book is released, I'd like to take it to schools, colleges and universities, sharing my story with young people that might be inspired by it. Whether it's the LGBT youth, people with learning difficulties or victims of bullying, if I can help just one person to see that - no matter how dark the struggle they are facing - there is light at the end of the tunnel, I'll be happy, and all of this will have been worthwhile.

One thing that I didn't anticipate, when I started out writing this book, was losing my mum. On the 30th June 2021, Mum had a stroke at home, and ended up being in hospital on her 60th birthday. She had planned a party for the 3rd of July, but it had to be rescheduled while she recovered. In the end, she spent two weeks in hospital before returning home to continue her recovery there. For a while, she seemed to be doing really well. She rebooked the party for the 18th September at the Latch Lifter in Ilkeston. We had a fantastic time with all of her friends and family: people were so happy to see Mum thriving, as well as to simply be surrounded by loved ones after such an extended period of lockdown. It was a truly brilliant evening.

The following day was the last time I saw Mum alive. She was in as cheerful a mood as I've ever seen her: she was laughing and joking, talking about future plans, and we parted on a happy note. The day after that - on the 20th September - Mum went into cardiac arrest at home. Unfortunately, she couldn't be saved, and we lost mum that evening. Her death has come as a big shock to all of her friends and family, and we've been devastated by her loss. RIP, Mum. I miss you every day. We all do.

I have to say though, Mum was very supportive of the idea of writing this book. I've dedicated it to her memory, and I know that if she were still here, she'd be so proud of what I've achieved. I do wish she could read the final version, but it helps to know that - if she were still here - she'd support me every step of the way. Mum may well be gone from this physical world, but I'm dedicating this book to her memory, and I intend to keep her spirit alive by raising money for the British Heart Foundation in her honour.

I'd like to end my story by offering some advice to my readers, which is simple enough but has helped me along the way: life is short so hold on to the people you love, go after the things that make you happy and don't forget to be yourself.

How I look without my glasses

Mine and my Dad's first holiday together - just the two of us in Blackpool!

I love you, Mum

StoryTerrace